# PERFECT
## APPRAISAL

**Terry O'Brien** is a best-selling author, columnist, consultant and motivational trainer. He is highly sought-after in the corporate as well as academic world, and has been training managers and providing counselling and consultancy over the past couple of decades. Author of hugely popular books on motivation, effective change and all that is 'un-Google-able', his writings focus on skill development and communication techniques. Terry O'Brien is a firm believer that 'infotainment' is a must for content to be effective, and his books are all about the three 'R's: Read, Record and Recall.

# PERFECT
## APPRAISAL

**Get it right every time**

*Terry O'Brien*

RUPA

Published by
Rupa Publications India Pvt. Ltd 2017
7/16, Ansari Road, Daryaganj
New Delhi 110002

*Sales centres:*
Allahabad Bengaluru Chennai
Hyderabad Jaipur Kathmandu
Kolkata Mumbai

Copyright © Terry O'Brien 2017

ISBN: 978-81-291-4543-7

First impression 2017

10 9 8 7 6 5 4 3 2 1

Typeset by Chetan Sharma

# Contents

# Introduction

A Performance Appraisal (PA), also known as performance review, performance evaluation, (career) development discussion or employee appraisal, is a method by which job performance of an employee is documented and evaluated. Performance appraisals are part of career development and consist of regular reviews of employees' performance within organisations. A performance appraisal is a systematic and periodic process that assesses an employee's performance and productivity. This is in relation to certain pre-established criteria and organisational objectives. Besides this, the other factors that count are organisational behaviour, accomplishments, potential for future improvement, strengths and weaknesses, etc.

There are three main methods to collect PA data.
- Objective production
- Personnel
- Judgemental evaluation

Performance appraisal helps the subordinates to answer two key questions.

- What is expected of me?
- How am I performing to meet these expectations?

Performance management systems are employed to manage and align all the resources of an organisation in order to achieve the highest possible performance. Indeed, improving employees' performance should be among the highest priorities, for everyone, for the betterment of the employees and the organisation.

### Applications Of Performance Appraisal

Compensation

Performance improvement

Promotion

Termination

Test validation

### Drawbacks

While there are many potential benefits of PA, there are also some potential drawbacks. PA may result in legal issues, if not executed appropriately, as many employees tend to be unsatisfied with the PA process.

An employee performance appraisal is a process—often combining both written and oral elements—whereby the management evaluates and provides feedback on the employee's performance including steps to improve or redirect activities, as needed. Documenting performance provides a basis for pay increase and promotion.

Appraisals are also important to help staff members improve their performance; they may be rewarded or recognised for a job well done. Besides this, they can serve as a launch point from which companies can clarify and shape responsibilities. Performance appraisal is supposed to be a developmental experience for the employees and a 'teaching moment' for managers.

## Performance Appraisal And Development

Here are the goals of an appraisal system.

- To improve the organisation's performance and results
- To make informed personnel decisions regarding promotion, job changes and termination
- To identify what is required to perform a job, such as goals and responsibilities
- To assess an employee's performance against these goals

In developing an appraisal system, the following need to be considered.

- Size of staff
- Employees on an alternate work schedule
- Goals of the organisation and desired employee behaviours to help achieve goals
- Measuring performance/work
- Pay increases and promotions

- Communication of appraisal system and individual performance
- Performance planning

The first cornerstone of appraisal is how to prepare, conduct and follow-up the joint discussions which are at the very heart of a perfect appraisal.

### *Appraisal schemes*

- Managers can get away with simply filling in forms on their staff and do not even have to show them what they have written, let alone talk to them about it (if they choose not to).
- Staff can get away with keeping their heads down; they may not even have to take an active part in their appraisals, if they do not want to.
- Both can, therefore, get away with paying lip service to the appraisal process, if it does not work for them.

However, if it has to be a 'perfect appraisal', they can't. It is the responsibility of both, managers and staff, to get together regularly to talk about work and to work out what is best for them and their organisation. This book offers a detailed concept for constructing this. Though not all appraisal schemes are based on managers conducting appraisals with individuals—for instance, team and peer appraisals—this is the most common scenario and the one taken here. It can also be the most difficult one to handle as well, as it involves putting the spotlight on two persons and their relationship.

*Perfect Appraisal* provides a simple method to accomplish this balance. It involves discussing assessment of people's performance, giving and taking criticism and praise, referring to weaknesses and strengths, talking about limitations and future potential, and in some cases even encouraging certain people to see that their future lies elsewhere.

This book deals with EPA (Employees' Performance Appraisal) and the six wise men of appraisal: 'Why', 'Who', 'Where', 'When', 'What' and 'How'.

If you have never taken part in appraisals before, try to equip yourself to do so. If you already have some experience with appraisals, then help yourself make them even better. This book is based on the premise of experience and learning; it makes little claim to originality or depth.

Indeed, here is all you need to get it right every time!

# Appraising Appraisal

Appraisal is an act of assessing something or someone. It has to be an impartial analysis and evaluation conducted according to established criteria to determine the acceptability, merit or worth of something or someone.

## TYPES OF APPRAISALS AND ASSESSMENT TERMS

### Traditional

In a traditional appraisal, the head of the institution or a manager sits down with an employee and discusses his/her performance for the previous performance period, usually a single year. The discussion is based on the manager's observations of the employee's abilities and performance of tasks as noted in the job description. The performance is rated, with the ratings tied to salary percentage increases. In addition, most traditional performance appraisal forms use too many rating categories and distribute ratings using a forced-distribution format. The appraisal form may use just three rating categories: outstanding, fully competent and unsatisfactory, as most managers can assess their best and worst employees, with the rest falling in between.

## Self-Appraisal

Self-appraisal is used in the performance appraisal process to encourage staff members to take responsibility for their performance by assessing their achievements or failures and promoting self-management of development goals. It also prepares employees to discuss these points with their managers. It may be used in conjunction with or as part of other appraisal processes, but it is not a substitute for the assessment of the employee's performance by a manager.

## Employee-initiated Reviews

In an employee-initiated review system, employees are informed that they can ask for a review by their manager. This type of on-demand appraisal is not meant to replace a conventional review process. It can be used to promote an attitude of self-management among workers.

Why it needs to be the *perfect* method from start to finish?

*There's so much good in the worst of us*

*and so much bad in the best of us*

*that it doesn't do for any of us*

*to sit and judge the rest of us*

Performance appraisal is a systematic evaluation of the performance of employees and an assessment of the potential of a person for further growth and development.

Performance appraisal is generally done in these ways.

- The supervisor evaluates the performance of employees and evaluates it with the targets and plans.

- The supervisor analyses the factors behind the work performances of employees.
- The employers are in a position to guide the employees towards better performance.

Don't think of a performance appraisal as an 'interview'. Do treat it as a discussion.

## Objectives Of Performance Appraisal

Performance appraisal can be done with these objectives in mind.

- To maintain records in order to determine compensation packages, wage structure and salary raises, etc.
- To identify the strengths and weaknesses of employees in order to place the right people in the right job
- To assess the potential in a person for further growth and development
- It can serve as the basis for influencing working habits of the employees
- It helps one to review and retain promotional and other training programmes

## Advantages Of Performance Appraisal

Performance appraisal is an investment for the company which can be justified by these advantages.

- **Promotion:** Performance appraisal helps the supervisors to chalk out promotion programmes for efficient employees. Also, inefficient workers can be dismissed or demoted.

- **Compensation:** Performance appraisal also helps in chalking out compensation packages for employees. Merit rating is possible through performance appraisal. It tries to give value to a performance. Compensation packages, which include bonus, high salary rates, extra benefits and allowances, are dependent on performance appraisal. The criterion should be merit rather than seniority.

- **Employee's development:** The systematic procedure of performance appraisal helps supervisors to frame training policies and programmes. It helps them to analyse the strengths and weaknesses of employees so that new jobs can be designed for efficient employees. It also helps in framing future development programmes.

- **Selection validation:** Performance appraisal helps the supervisors to understand the validity and importance of the selection procedure. The supervisors come to know the validity and thereby the strengths and weaknesses of the selection procedure. Changes in selection methods can be made in this regard.

- **Communication:** For an organisation, effective communication between employees and employers is very important. Through performance appraisal, communication can be made in these ways.

  - Employers can understand and accept the skills of the subordinates.

  - Subordinates can also understand and create trust and confidence in superiors.

  - It also helps in maintaining a cordial and congenial labour-management relationship.

- It develops the spirit of work and boosts the morale of employees.
- **Motivation:** Performance appraisal serves as a motivational tool. Through evaluating performance of employees, a person's efficiency can be determined. This, very well, motivates a person for doing better and helps him to improve his performance in the future.

The perfect appraisal is about people frequently meeting to discuss how things are going at work and how they could do even better in the future.

## DO JUSTICE TO IT

### Find The Right Words

Sometimes, for employees, the word 'appraisal' itself can have negative connotations. Is it not, after all, an assessment of their performance? They may feel vulnerable and defensive at the idea that someone will be passing judgement on them. In order to avoid this misconception, it may be helpful to describe the process in a way which more accurately suggests its purpose.

- Performance improvement and development
- Progress and planning
- Joint review and action planning
- Investing in people

The perfect appraisal should be seen to be what it is: positive rather than negative; constructive rather than destructive; and forward-looking rather than backward-looking.

## Do It More Frequently

Bearing in mind the number of work-related events that occur annually and require your attention as a manager (everything from pay reviews to organising office annual parties), it is easy to assume that appraisal is just another chore that needs to be done, once every year. Rather, it should be an ongoing process. Even with staff, who you feel require little supervision and guidance, and who may need no more than one comprehensive appraisal of their 'world of work' per year, you will need to undertake regular and frequent 'mini' appraisals that look at:

- how the job is going.
- how they are doing.
- how they can develop.
- what you can do to make it happen.

Don't include it with salary or disciplinary matters. Handle these matters separately. To introduce such issues at the appraisal will completely destroy its credibility as a 'helping' rather than 'judging' process. It would be absurd to assume that staff will be prepared to discuss their performance and shortcomings in an open and objective way, when they feel that their financial rewards are at stake.

Pay reviews and appraisals should be kept several months apart, so that staff can satisfy themselves that the two are not directly linked. Similarly, where merit payments or performance-related bonuses are given, the staff members will have both the incentive and opportunity to act on the results of the appraisal.

Disciplinary issues, in any event, will need to follow a different set of procedures. Where disciplinary procedures already exist, it will be well to defer the appraisal until their outcome is clear. Don't let other people get the wrong impression.

## Stress What It Is All About

It is most important that employees approach an appraisal in a positive frame of mind or at least with an open mind. Care should be taken to present the process as a means of:

- learning from the past and as an aid to the future.
- recognising abilities and potential.
- developing the required knowledge, skills and attitude.
- building on successes and overcoming difficulties.
- increasing motivation and job satisfaction.
- enhancing relationships and fostering teamwork.

Don't play it by ear.

## Plan Thoroughly

Effective preparation has a vital role to play in the success of any business meeting and this is particularly true of a perfect appraisal. An ill-prepared manager sends a negative signal to the subject of the appraisal. The inference is that the staff member involved is not worthy of more than cursory individual consideration. Quite aside from this demotivating aspect is the obvious inequity of one, albeit senior, who has not done his/her job properly coming to discuss the apparent shortcomings of another.

Nevertheless, thorough preparation certainly does not mean setting up a formal and elaborate 'appraisal system', as this approach will merely contribute to misgivings and apprehensions about the process. Rather, it is addressing these basic questions—Why? Who? Where? When? What? How? —in readiness for a 'meeting of minds'.

## ENCOURAGE EVERYONE

Don't be the only one to plan.

### Give It A Thought

Preparation is important for both sides. Encouraging staff members' involvement in this way will increase their motivation and sense of 'ownership' for their work. The perfect appraisal should be a collaborative venture between the management and staff.

**Remember:** One-sided planning leads to one-sided discussion and, eventually, one-sided outcomes.

### *Do try it out*

Managers and staff, alike, tend to fight shy of appraisals; little wonder, given the sensitivities involved and the careful thought needed to handle them sensitively. The perfect appraisal, however, can be one of the most rewarding experiences for managers, their staff and the organisations in which they work. It is about enabling people to give their very best to their work and get the very best from it. So do give it a try.

## PERFORMANCE APPRAISAL

It is the process by which a manager or consultant:

- examines and evaluates an employee's work and behaviour by comparing it with preset standards.
- documents the results of the comparison.
- uses the results to provide feedback to the employee to show where improvement is needed and why.

Performance appraisals are employed to determine who needs what training and who will be promoted, demoted, retained or fired.

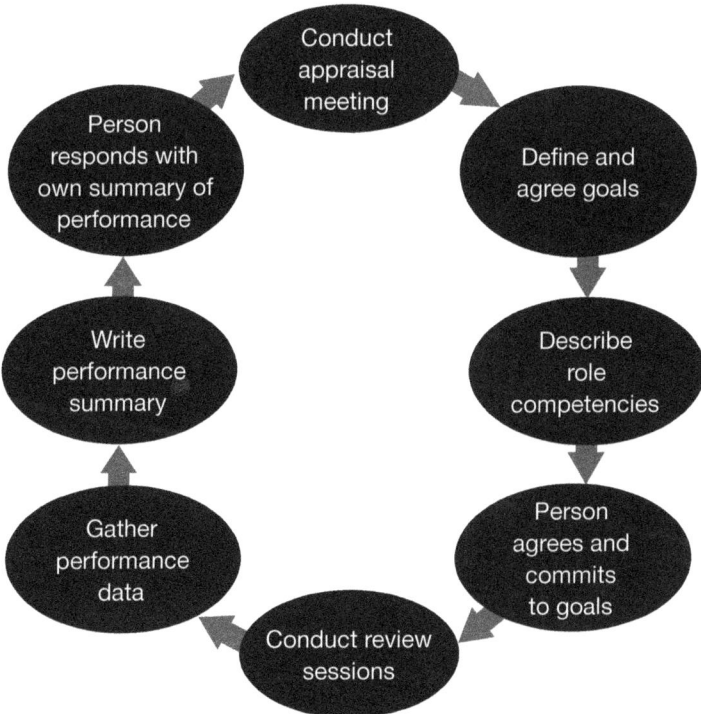

Conduct appraisal meeting → Define and agree goals → Describe role competencies → Person agrees and commits to goals → Conduct review sessions → Gather performance data → Write performance summary → Person responds with own summary of performance

# 2

# Appraisal: Key Part Of Performance Management System

The history of appraisals goes back to the third century AD in China. It is a tool that has stood the test of time and has increased in popularity in the recent years. If used sensitively, it can be extremely valuable to employees and teams.

Performance appraisal is necessary. It is a means to assess an employee's current and/or past performance relative to his or her performance standards. This process involves three steps.

- Setting work standards
- Evaluating performance accordingly
- Giving feedback for continuous professional development

The question is 'why' is it needed.

- It is a fact that most employers still base pay, promotion and retention decisions on their employees' appraisal.

- Performance appraisal plays a pivotal role in performance management, which is about continuous improvement, being goal-oriented and evaluating how well an employee's or team's performance conforms to the company's overall goals.
- It helps correct any weak links and capitalises on things done well.
- Career planning becomes easier. One can mould one's career in accordance with his or her exhibited strengths and weaknesses.
- It helps identify employees' training and development (cause and remedy) needs, especially if there is a 'performance gap'.

## PERFORMANCE APPRAISAL

Appraisal is a step towards brilliance. It is not to spell out spite. Appraisals are a means for taking stock of achievements and setting the agenda for future action. They are means to periodically focus on our performance and discuss it in confidence. Employers see appraisals as a key part of a 'performance management system' designed to ensure that employees are in tune with the developments in the business. Appraisal also ensure that individuals and teams are managed well to achieve high level of output.

It is believed by many that appraisals encourage people to link their performance to the objectives of the organisation and respond to increased competition within the industry.

The most effective way of appraisal is to take a holistic approach to this exercise. Some would prefer appraisals to

# Performance Appraisal Form

Date: _____

Employee Name: _____

Employee ID #: _____

Position: _____

Current salary: _____

Date of next review: _____

| Performance Category | Scores | Remarks |
| --- | --- | --- |
| Ability at the position | | |
| Attendance | | |
| Leadership ability | | |
| Ability to meet deadlines | | |
| Organisational skills | | |
| Quality of work | | |
| Teamwork ability | | |
| Team player abilities | | |

Future goals discussed: _____

_____

Supervisor/Appraiser comments: _____

_____

Employee comments: _____

_____

*Supervisor/Appraiser Signatures:* _____

*Employee Signatures:* _____

be confidential between employees and their manager. But a healthy open-arm appraisal involves getting the views of several people whose work relates to the employee, who's performance is being evaluated. Such appraisals can be open to customers and suppliers as well as colleagues. Administratively, this is more difficult as it requires the collection of many different views, but it does highlight the problems that occur, especially if key people are unhappy with particular behaviours.

From an employee's perspective, it is a good measure of the achievement of the goals that have been set, preferably through discussion with managers and to discuss new goals that need to be addressed during the coming time. These new requirements may arise due to a change in circumstances, such as alterations in how the business is run and staff changes that bring different responsibilities.

Managers, like those they manage, often dislike appraising their staff. Appraisals work best if the appraiser has received training in how to conduct them. Often, staff members are required to complete a form before their appraisal and with their appraiser. They may be asked to assess for themselves their level of achievement over the preceding period and indicate what they have learned or skills they have developed.

The process of positive appraisal is not retrogressive; it is progressive. It is a means to look forward. Keeping this in mind, appraisal forms may ask employees to consider what their objectives are for the coming period and to make proposals—what they might achieve, what support might they require and what additional resources will be necessary.

A useful tool when setting objectives is the acronym **'SMART'.**
The goals should be:

- **S**pecific
- **M**easurable
- **A**chievable
- **R**ealistic
- **T**ime bound

Detractors of **'SMART'** use the acronym **'DUMB'**

- **D**efective
- **O**utdated
- **M**isdirected
- **B**ureaucratic

The truth is that in many organisations and situations, time-sensitive goal setting is a way to progress. 'March forward; fare forward' ought to be the mantra.

An important aspect of appraisal is training and development requirements. Indeed, the only permanent thing is change—new situations arise, organisations change direction and technology moves on. We cannot rely on the skills we already have to see us through. Inevitably, there is a need for training and identifying it as a valuable part of this discussion.

Performance appraisals are essential for effective management and evaluation of staff. Appraisals help to develop individuals, improve organisational performance and formulate business plans. Formal performance appraisals are generally conducted annually for all staff in an organisation. Each staff member is appraised by his/her line manager. Directors are appraised by the CEO, who is appraised by the chairman or company owners, depending on the size and structure of the organisation.

Annual performance appraisals enable management to monitor standards, agree upon expectations and objectives, and delegate responsibilities and tasks. Staff performance appraisals also help in identifying training needs and addressing them.

Performance appraisals also typically feed into pay and grading reviews, which commonly coincide with business planning for the next trading year.

Performance appraisals generally review each individual's performance against the objectives and standards for the current trading year, agreed upon at the previous appraisal meeting.

Performance appraisals are also essential for career and succession planning for individuals, crucial functions and for the organisation as a whole.

Performance appraisals are important for staff motivation, attitude, behaviour development and aligning individual and organisational aims. Performance appraisals provide a formal, recorded and regular review of an individual's performance and a plan for future development.

Job performance appraisals—in whatever form—are, therefore, vital for managing the performance of individuals and organisations.

Appraisals are much easier, and more relaxed, if the boss meets each of the team members individually and regularly for one-to-one discussions throughout the year.

## Social Responsibility And Development

Appraisals include accountabilities relating to **corporate responsibility**. This includes the 'triple bottom line'—Profit-People-Planet, corporate social responsibility (CSR), sustainability, corporate integrity and ethics, and fair trade, etc. The organisation must decide the extent to which these accountabilities are reflected in job responsibilities, which would then feature accordingly in performance appraisals. Appraisals must address 'complete person' development and not just job skills or the skills required for the next promotion.

And above all, appraisals must not discriminate against anyone on the grounds of age, gender, sexual orientation, race, religion and disability, etc.

## Developing The 'Complete Person'

When designing/planning and conducting appraisals, seek to help the 'complete person' by providing trainings for overall development and not limiting them to the required/relevant work skills. Increasingly, the best employers recognise that growing the 'complete person' promotes positive attitude. It is also an important aspect of modern corporate responsibility.

## Performance Appraisals Are Beneficial

Think about everything that performance appraisals can achieve and contribute to, when they are properly managed, such as:

- performance measurement—transparent; short-, medium- and long-term.

- clarifying, defining and redefining priorities and objectives.
- motivation through achievement and feedback.
- training needs and learning desires—assessment and agreement.
- identification of personal strengths.
- role clarification and team building.
- resolving confusions and misunderstandings.

Performance appraisals of all types are effective if they are conducted properly, and better still if the appraisal process is clearly explained and agreed to by the people involved.

**Warning:** Review informally and often.

This removes much of the pressure for managers and appraisees at formal appraisal time. Leaving everything to a single make-or-break discussion once a year is asking for trouble.

Well-prepared and well-conducted performance appraisals provide unique opportunities to appraisees and managers to improve and develop.

## METHODS OF EVALUATION

Aside from formal traditional (annual, six-monthly, quarterly or monthly) performance appraisals, there are many different methods of performance evaluation. The use of any of these methods depends on the purpose of the evaluation, the individual, the assessor and the environment.

The formal annual performance appraisal is generally the over-riding instrument which reviews all other performance data for the previous year.

Performance appraisals should be a positive experience. The appraisal process provides a platform for development and motivation. So organisations should foster among employees the feeling that performance appraisals are positive opportunities, in order to get the best out of the people and the process.

Types of performance and aptitude assessments:

- Formal annual performance appraisals
- Probationary reviews
- Informal one-to-one review discussions
- Counselling meetings
- Observation on the job
- Skill- or job-related tests

Holding regular informal one-to-one review meetings greatly reduces the pressure and time required for the annual formal appraisal meeting. Holding informal reviews every month is ideal for all staff.

## PERFORMANCE APPRAISAL PROCESS

### Prepare

Prepare all material—notes, agreed tasks and records of performance, achievements, incidents and reports—pertaining to performance and achievement.

## Inform

Inform the appraisee—ensure that the appraisee is informed of the time, purpose and type of appraisal.

## Venue

Ensure that a suitable venue, which would be free from interruptions, is identified.

## Layout

Room layout and seating are also important elements to prepare. Don't simply accept whatever layout happens to exist in a room. Layout has a huge influence on the atmosphere and mood.

## Introduction

Relax the appraisee. Open with a positive statement; smile; be warm and friendly. The appraisee may be terrified; it's your responsibility to create a calm and non-threatening atmosphere.

## Review And Measure

Review the activities, tasks, objectives and achievements one by one; avoid tangents or vague and unspecific topics.

## Agree On An Action Plan

An overall plan should be agreed with the appraisee, which should take account of the job responsibilities, the appraisee's career aspirations, the departmental and organisational priorities and the reviewed strengths and weaknesses.

## Agree Specific Objectives

These are the specific actions and targets that together form the action plan. Adhere to rules that are SMARTER: Specific, Measurable, Agreed, Realistic, Time-bound, Enjoyable and Recorded.

## Agree Upon The Necessary Support

This is the support required for the appraisee to achieve the objectives.

Also consider training and development that relates to 'complete person' development outside of job skills. This might be a hobby or a talent that the person wants to develop. Developing a person in this way will bring benefits to their role and will increase motivation and loyalty. The best employers understand the value of helping the whole person to develop.

## Invite Any Other Points Or Questions

Make sure you capture any other concerns.

## Close Positively

Thank the appraisee for their contribution to the meeting and their effort through the year, and commit to help in any way you can.

## Format

The format should include appraisee's name, date, feedback respondent's name, designation and guidelines for completion, etc.

| Question number | Feedback question | Key skill/capability | Skill/capability |
|---|---|---|---|
| 1 | | | |
| 2 | | | |
| 3 | | | |
| 4 | | | |
| 5 | | | |
| 6 | | | |
| 7 | | | |
| 8 | | | |
| 9 | | | |
| 10 | | | |
| 11 | | | |
| 12 | | | |
| 13 | | | |
| 14 | | | |
| 15 | | | |
| 16 | | | |

| | | | |
|---|---|---|---|
| 17 | | | |
| 18 | | | |
| 19 | | | |
| 20 | | | |
| 21 | | | |
| 22 | | | |
| 23 | | | |
| 24 | | | |
| 25 | | | |
| 26 | | | |
| 27 | | | |
| 28 | | | |
| 29 | | | |
| 30 | | | |

**Optional section:** Additional feedback (If you provide this option, it is advisable to ask the respondents to be as constructive/comprehensive as possible.)

# 3

## A Holistic Approach

It is easy to assume that the best judge of performance is the line manager or supervisor. This may not be true. A holistic approach is the best. Good information about performance is likely to come from all sorts of sources—line manager, supervisor, the employee, colleagues and production figures, etc. A really effective appraisal system will make use of as many of these information sources as is practicable.

The best source of information about employee performance may often be the employee himself or herself. Obtaining information can be done jointly by the employee and the supervisor or manager in a formal or informal interview, or solely by the employee. It may be that people are not completely honest about their own performance, so managers tend to doubt employees' abilities to rate themselves. This may be reluctance by the manager to give up perceived authority. The next source of performance information is peers. Peer appraisal is potentially more accurate as they spend more time with the person being appraised than the managers. Relationships between peers, however, may mean that such information is not accurately presented. Peers may be on the defensive.

They may give inaccurate information for reasons of their own. Finally, where employees are in contact with customers and suppliers, performance information may come from those individuals who the employee regularly deals with. This may take the form of customer service enquiries or customer feedback documents.

The appraiser may be any person who observes the employee while performing a job and has thorough knowledge about the job content, contents to be appraised and standards of contents. The appraiser should be capable of determining what is more important and what is relatively less important. He should prepare reports and make judgements without bias. Typical appraisers are supervisors, peers, subordinates, employees themselves and users of services and consultants.

## STAKEHOLDERS

### Supervisors

Supervisors include the employee's immediate superiors or other superiors having knowledge about the work of the employee and the departmental head/manager. The general practice is that immediate superiors appraise the performance, which in turn, is reviewed by the departmental head/manager. This is because supervisors are responsible for managing their subordinates and they have the opportunity to observe, direct and control their subordinates continuously. Moreover, they are accountable for the performance of their subordinates. Sometimes other supervisors, who have close contact with the employee's work also appraise with a view to provide additional information.

## Peers

Peer appraisal may be reliable if the work group is stable over a reasonably long period of time and performs tasks that require interaction.

**Note:** More often than not in business organisations, if employees were to be evaluated by their peers, the whole exercise may degenerate into a popularity contest, paving way for the impairment of work relationships.

## Subordinates

The concept of having superiors rated by subordinates is being used in most organisations today. For instance, in most technical and professional universities, students evaluate a professor's performance in the classroom. Such a novel method can be useful in other organisational settings too, provided the relationships between superiors and subordinates are cordial. Subordinates' ratings in such cases can be quite useful in identifying competent superiors. Though useful in universities and research institutions, this approach may not gain acceptance in traditional organisations where subordinates practically do not enjoy much discretion.

## Self-appraisal

Employee development means self-development; employees who appraise their own performance may become highly motivated. If individuals understand the objectives they are expected to achieve and the standards by which they are to be evaluated, they are (to a great extent) in the best position to appraise their own performance.

## Users Of Services

Employees' performance in service organisations relating to behaviours, promptness, speed in doing the job and accuracy can be better judged by the customers or users of services. For example, a teacher's performance is better judged by students and the performance of a cab service provider is better judged by passengers.

## Consultants

Sometimes, consultants may be engaged for appraisal when employees or employers do not trust the supervisory appraisal and management does not trust self-appraisal, peer appraisal or subordinate appraisal. In this situation, consultants are engaged.

In order to plug holes, if any, several organisations follow a multiple rating system wherein several superiors separately fill out rating forms on the same subordinate.

# 4

# The Performance Appraisal Interview

The performance appraisal interview consists of three stages.

- Preparing for the appraisal
- Conducting the appraisal
- Following up

## PREPARING FOR THE APPRAISAL

Time is an important factor. Enough time should be given, both to the appraiser and the appraisee, to prepare thoroughly.

A number of things need to be done in preparation to ensure a fruitful discussion.

### Review Is A Must

Review the appraisees' performance appraisal forms to refresh your memory regarding performance measures—goals, objectives, KPIs and competencies—that were agreed with them. Review their previous appraisal summary and Performance Optimisation Plans (POPs) to see what was agreed that they should work on improving. Study their performance record notes accumulated throughout the performance period. Consult all other relevant records on their performance.

It has to be a two-way process. Inform them to prepare for the appraisal by completing and printing out their performance appraisal forms, and study/print their performance record notes. The system allows you to request that they release their forms to you, prior to the appraisal.

A time, date and place must be mutually agreed upon for the interview. A minimum of one week's notice should be given. For more senior and specialist positions, allow even more preparation time.

**Venue Factor**

The venue is equally crucial. Select a venue where you can meet in a relaxed, unhurried and informal atmosphere without disturbances or interruptions. Avoid sitting behind a desk during the interview. Rather, sit together with the appraisee in front of your desk or, alternatively, at a conference table. Sitting behind a desk transmits a non-verbal message of formality, reinforcing the superior-subordinate relationship. Such demarcations should be obliterated.

**Time Factor**

Set aside adequate time for the appraisal interview, which may vary in length from 45–90 minutes, depending on the complexity and seniority of the appraisees' positions.

# CONDUCTING THE APPRAISAL

The performance appraisal consists of two distinct parts: 'Then' and 'Hereafter'.

**Reviewing performance:** Look 'backwards' at how well the previously-set performance measures and standards were achieved, and the factors that affected them.

**Planning performance:** Look 'forward' at the new or adapted performance measures and standards to be achieved during the next performance period.

Here are five steps that need to be followed to ensure a constructive session.

- Start with an icebreaker—this enables one to relax and not be stressed
- Explain the purpose of the interview—the goal is important
- Work through the performance measures (actual performance, ratings and POPs)
- Jointly set performance measures and standards for the next performance period
- Close on a positive note—what is said at the end is what one takes home

## Step 1: Start With An Icebreaker

Start the discussion with a small talk to ease the initial tension of the interview. It should not be anything to do with work; more of an informal talk. This will ease the situation.

**Step 2: Explain The Purpose Of The Interview**

Explaining how you wish to conduct the appraisal interview will let appraisees know what to expect and it will also eliminate any unrealistic fears they may have.

**Step 3: Work Through The Performance Measures**

*Agreeing actual performance—be the facilitator*

Take the performance measures one at a time and ask the appraisee how he/she has done on them. Ask for and give facts and 'evidence' pertaining to each. (Consult the appraisee's performance record notes.)

Your job is to act as a facilitator of the process. Always ask for the appraisee's comments first. The key is to get them to self-appraise. Ask probing questions to get examples and supporting evidence of good performance. If you disagree, don't say so directly—rather ask questions so that appraisees can come to more realistic conclusions themselves. Try necessitating the opinion of the appraisee even more than yours.

Praise them where deserved (be genuine and sincere) and mention specific examples of achievement and behaviour.

For example:

- You do contribute a lot to the organisation…
- I am particularly pleased with the way you…
- Your contribution here means that we…

When discussing performance measures that have not been sufficiently met, it becomes even more important for appraisees to self-appraise. It is so much more effective if they mention areas for improvement themselves. People can also sometimes be much harder on themselves than others would be.

Explore the factors that have affected their performance. Probe:

- Why?
- What happened?
- What would have helped?
- How can we correct the situation/prevent it from happening again?

Using 'we' as opposed to 'you' in trying to find solutions to problems indicates to appraisees that they are not alone in this and that your support is always available.

Be careful not to shift the blame. Discuss performance, not personality. Focus on performance improvement and actions to prevent the recurrence of problems. There is nothing you or anyone else can do any more about the past. Rather use the lessons from the past to improve on the future. Concentrate on behaviour that can be changed and give praise where possible—even when discussing poor performance.

Avoid negative words such as 'not up to the mark', 'mistakes', 'sloppy', 'careless' and 'shortcomings'. The key is to keep your feedback constructive and non-judgemental. Do try to maintain the appraisee's self-esteem throughout.

Admit openly if you have a shared responsibility for the appraisee's under-performance and undertake to set this right. Also, admit if you are wrong in your interpretation of the facts.

If they blame you for something that went wrong, stay calm and avoid defending yourself—respond in a non-reactive way and don't get personal. Avoid arguments by focusing on facts and supporting evidence. Always avoid comparisons with other people.

Don't allow appraisees to avoid their areas of under-performance. Attempt to make them admit to these with probing questions. If they persist in avoiding certain issues, give it to them straight, but sensitively, for instance, 'Jyoti, let's now talk about the three letters of customer complaint we have received over this performance period. How do you feel about that?'

### *Rating performance*

After each performance measure has been discussed and the agreed actual performance notes recorded, the appraiser and appraisee need to give it a realistic performance rating. For this purpose, use the rating key/scale performance standards and/or behavioural indicators listed in the performance appraisal form for each measure.

**Rating scale:** Don't give your own preliminary ratings (even if the appraisee asks for it). Rather ask the appraisee what he/she thinks would be a fair rating based on actual performance as agreed and recorded. If the rating is unrealistically high, facilitate a more realistic rating by asking questions, such as:

- 'Considering the three customer complaints you have received, Jyoti, how do you justify a 4-rating—"Above target/standard"?'

**Directions:** Complete this form by circling the number that most closely corresponds to your observations of the employee. Do this on at least two different occasions.

**Scale:**
1=Poor   2=Below Average   3=Average   4=Above Average
5=Excellent

| | | | | | |
|---|---|---|---|---|---|
| Quality of work: | 1 | 2 | 3 | 4 | 5 |
| Knowledge of job: | 1 | 2 | 3 | 4 | 5 |
| Communication skills: | 1 | 2 | 3 | 4 | 5 |
| Interpersonal skills: | 1 | 2 | 3 | 4 | 5 |

**Total** _____

**Date:** _____ **Name of Employee:** _____

**Supervisor's Signature:** _____

- 'Considering the number of customer complaints you have received, Jyoti, how do you justify a 3-rating—"On target/standard, including small deviations plus or minus"? I cannot agree that three such, rather serious, complaints be regarded as small negative deviations. What do you think?'

Be prepared to adjust your thinking on a rating if the facts and arguments offered justify it.

Good care must be taken that the rating of performance does not become a battle of wits. The correct parameter is to stick to actual performance as proven by performance data/statistics and recorded incidents/evidence (as discussed with the employee).

Both parties should also approach the appraisal process in a positive and constructive spirit so that the management and appraisees can effectively deliver on their intended purpose.

The primary aim of a performance appraisal is to identify stumbling blocks that prevented the appraisee from performing optimally. Thus, this ought to be open to discussion in order to achieve just that. The rating of performance is secondary and should not detract from the problem-solving purpose of the discussion.

### Completing the POPs

Performance measures and standards that have not been met, need to be put back on track. Engage in joint problem-solving to do so, as each performance measure is discussed. The result of this discussion is recorded in the POP field of each performance measure on the performance appraisal form.

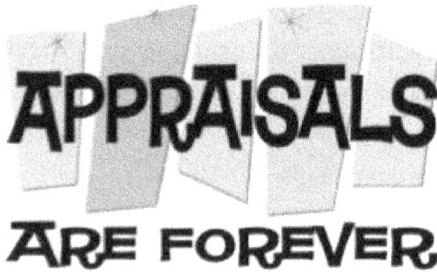

APPRAISALS ARE FOREVER

Staff training and coaching (as per the traditional personal development plan) are seldom the only solutions for addressing unacceptable performance or behaviour.

Poor performance or behaviour can be due to a lack of resources and work tools, poor systems, policies and procedures, poor rewards and recognition practices, insufficient performance feedback, poor management practices, and a generally counter-productive working environment and organisation culture. Be open-minded to consider and address all of these, along with employee training and development. The result will be continuous performance improvement, organisational development and proactive change in the management, leading to a 'learning organisation' in the true sense of the word.

## Step 4: Agree Performance Measures And Standards For The Next Performance Period

This is the 'forward-looking' section of the interview as mentioned above. This part of the discussion can be held right now as the 'second half' of the interview or as a separate session within the next week or two. It is crucial that new or adapted performance measures and standards be discussed and documented as close as possible to the start of the new performance period, so that the employee has the maximum possible time to deliver on them.

Also discuss any support you need to give employees. Support is all about minimising environmental barriers to performance, providing employees with the necessary resources, training and coaching opportunities, and motivating them.

## Step 5: Close On A Positive Note

Make a positive closing statement, reiterating your appreciation of the appraisee's efforts, assuring him/her of your trust in their abilities and future performance, for instance, 'Jyoti, thank you for the frank and constructive way in which you have approached this. I would just like to end by thanking you once again for the effort you have put in over the last few months and also to assure you of my full trust in your abilities to tackle your new objectives and targets competently. Please be rest assured of my commitment to support you where I can…and please do not hesitate to speak to me as and when needed.'

## FOLLOW UP

### Managing By Walking Around

The performance agreement for the next performance period can be viewed as a negotiated contract. Appraisees are committing themselves to achieve certain objectives/targets in return for specified support from their line managers. It is crucial that you deliver on this promised support.

- Provide all possible psychological (praise, recognition and encouragement) and physical support (work tools, equipment, finances and staff).

- Show interest; be where the action is; observe their performance; enquire about progress; and offer assistance.

- Arrange the necessary training and coaching as identified.

- Provide regular feedback on performance (both positive and negative/constructive) as soon as possible after the event.

- Create a pleasant working environment and climate where people can fulfil their social and other motivational needs, while maintaining a business focus and urgency.

## Firmness Of Manner

You do need a certain firmness of manner, which should be used as required during the appraisal. It is your job to keep the interview on track and not allow major digressions. Do not accept any ideas or suggestions from appraisees that you are not fully satisfied with or that are not congruent with corporate and your own goals and standards. Tell them what these non-negotiable parameters are that you cannot compromise on.

**Note:** Firmness of manner means assertiveness, not aggression. It means ensuring you stay in control of the interview—always politely, but with authority.

## Confidentiality

The appraisee must be able to trust you to keep whatever is discussed confidentially.

### *Fair assessment: External factors affecting performance*

In assessing an appraisee's performance, the extent to which circumstances beyond their control have influenced the achievement of their objectives, must be taken into consideration. If these circumstances have contributed greatly to good results, they should not get the benefit of it. Likewise, they should not be punished if adverse, uncontrollable causes have prevented them from achieving their objectives optimally.

The quality of an employee's performance also frequently depends on how good, reliable and consistent he/she is at work.

Can the non-achievement of objectives also possibly be ascribed to the fact that other objectives took priority over it at some point?

Also ask yourself to what extent the performance environment (organisation's culture, policies, rules, systems, structure, infrastructure and resources, etc.) has prevented appraisees from achieving their goals.

### Appraisal pitfalls

These need to be borne in mind during the performance rating process.

- Tendency to give all employees more or less the same ratings, or giving an employee the same rating on all his/her performance measures (to avoid potential conflict)
- Consistently being too strict or too lenient
- Don't give higher ratings to certain employees based on your personal preferences or one-off incidents instead of actual performance over the entire period
- Managers should differentiate very clearly between those employees who achieved their objectives and those who did not, and give clear messages to both. 'Compromising' and giving all employees the same bonus or increment will send the wrong message to everybody. Top performers will feel punished (even cheated) and poor performers will be rewarded.

- Managers must have the courage to give credit where it is due and not be manipulated by those poor performers who rather bet on the manager's fear of confrontation. Such managers invariably end up losing the respect and loyalty of both types of performers.

# 5

# The Appraisal Process

The last step in the appraisal process is preparing a final report of value. This report will provide you and your appraisee with a complete analysis. It will outline how the appraiser calculated your work.

Performance appraisal is the assessment of an individual's performance in a systematic way. It is a developmental tool used for all-round development of an employee and the organisation. The performance is measured against factors, such as job knowledge, quality and quantity of output, initiative, leadership abilities, supervision, dependability, cooperation, judgement, versatility and health. Assessment should be confined to past as well as potential performance. The second definition is more focused on behaviours as part of assessment because behaviours do affect job results.

**Performance appraisals and job analysis relationship**

| Job Analysis | Performance Standards | Performance Appraisals |
|---|---|---|
| Describe the work and requirements of a particular job | Translate job requirements into levels of acceptable or unacceptable performance | Describe the relevant strengths and weaknesses of each individual |

## Uses Of Performance Appraisal

- Promotions
- Confirmations
- Training and development
- Compensation reviews
- Competency building
- Improving communication
- Evaluation of HR programmes
- Feedback and grievances

## Goals of performance appraisals

| General Goals | Specific Goals |
|---|---|
| Developmental uses | Individual needs |
| | Performance feedback |
| | Transfers and placements |
| | Strengths and development needs |
| Administrative uses | Salary |
| | Promotion |
| | Retention/Termination |
| | Recognition |
| | Lay-offs |
| | Poor performers identification |

| | |
|---|---|
| Organisational maintenance | HR planning |
| | Training needs |
| | Achievements of organisational goals |
| | Goal identification |
| | HR systems evaluation |
| | Reinforcement of organisational needs |
| Documentation | Validation research |
| | For HR decisions |
| | Legal requirements |

## Performance Appraisal Process

- Stating the objectives
- Stating the expectations
- Designing an appraisal programme
- Performance appraisal
- Performance interviews
- Using data for appropriate purposes
- Identifying opportunities and variables
- Providing the necessary assistance

## Traditional and modern approach to appraisals

| Categories | Traditional Appraisals | Modern Systems Appraisals |
|---|---|---|
| Guiding values | Individualistic; control oriented; documentary | Systematic; developmental; problem-solving |
| Leadership styles | Directional; evaluative | Facilitative; coaching |
| Frequency | Occasional | Frequent |
| Formalities | High | Low |
| Rewards | Individualistic | Grouped; organisational |

## TECHNIQUES/METHODS OF QUANTITY AND QUALITY PERFORMANCE APPRAISALS

Numerous methods have been devised to measure the quantity and quality of performance appraisals. Each of these methods is effective only for some purposes and for some organisations. None should be dismissed or accepted as appropriate except as they relate to the particular needs of the organisation or an employee.

The methods of appraisal can be divided into two categories.

- Past-oriented methods
- Future-oriented methods

## Past-oriented Methods

### *Rating scales*

Rating scales consist of several numerical scales representing job-related performance criteria, such as dependability, initiative, output, attendance and attitude, etc. Each scale ranges from 'Excellent' to 'Poor'. The total numerical scores are computed and conclusions derived.

**Advantages:** It is adaptable, easy to use and cost effective; every type of job can be evaluated; a large number of employees can be covered; and no formal training is required.

**Disadvantages:** Biases

### *Checklist*

Under this method, a checklist for traits of employees, in the form of 'Yes' or 'No' based questions, is prepared. Here, the rater only does the reporting or checking while the HR department does the actual evaluation.

**Advantages:** It is standardised, economic, easily administered and limited training is required.

**Disadvantages:** Biases; use of improper evaluation by the HR, does not allow rater to give relative ratings

### Forced choice method

The statements are arranged in blocks of two or more and the rater indicates which statement is true or false. The rater is forced to make a choice. The HR department does the actual assessment.

**Advantages:** Absence of personal biases because of forced choice.

**Disadvantages:** Statements may be wrongly framed.

### Forced distribution method

Here, employees are clustered around a high point on a rating scale. Rater is compelled to distribute the employees on all points on the scale. It is assumed that the performance is conformed to normal distribution.

**Advantages:** Eliminates

**Disadvantages:** Assumption of normal distribution is unrealistic.

### Critical incidents method

This approach is focused on certain critical behaviours of employees that make all the difference in the performance. Supervisors record such incidents as and when they occur.

**Advantages:** Evaluations are based on actual job behaviours; ratings are supported by descriptions; feedback is easy; reduces biases; and chances of subordinate improvement are high.

**Disadvantages:** Negative incidents can be prioritised; incidents can be overlooked; overly close supervision; feedback may be too much and may appear to be a punishment.

### Behaviourally anchored rating scales

Statements of effective and ineffective behaviours determine the points. They are behaviourally anchored. The rater is supposed to say, which behaviour describes the employee's performance.

**Advantages:** It helps in preventing rating errors.

**Disadvantages:** It suffers from distortions inherent in most rating techniques.

### Field review method

This is an appraisal done by someone outside the employees' own department, usually from corporate or the HR department.

**Advantages:** It is useful for managerial-level promotions, when comparable information is needed.

**Disadvantages:** Outsider is generally not familiar with employees work environment; observation of actual behaviours is not possible.

### Performance tests and observations

This is based on the test of knowledge or skills. The tests may be written or an actual presentation of skills. Tests must be reliable and validated to be useful.

**Advantage:** Tests may be made to measure potential.

**Disadvantages:** Tests may suffer if cost of test development or administration is high.

### Confidential records

Mostly used by government departments, however, their application in industry is not ruled out. Here, the report is given in the form of an Annual Confidentiality Report (ACR) and may record the ratings with respect to these items: attendance, self-expression, teamwork, leadership, initiative, technical ability, reasoning ability, originality and resourcefulness, etc.

**Advantages:** The system is highly secretive and confidential; feedback is given only in case of an adverse entry.

**Disadvantage:** Highly subjective and ratings can be manipulated because the evaluations are linked to HR actions like promotions etc.

### Essay method

In this method, the rater writes down the employee's description, in detail, in broad categories like overall impression, promote-ability, existing capabilities, strengths, weaknesses and training needs.

**Advantage:** It is extremely useful in filling information gaps about employees that often occur in a better-structured checklist.

**Disadvantage:** It is highly dependent on the writing skills of the rater; success depends on the memory power of raters.

### Cost accounting method

Here, performance is evaluated on the basis of monetary returns to the organisation.

**Advantages:** The cost to keep the employee and the benefit the organisation derives therefore is ascertained.

**Disadvantages:** It is dependent on cost and benefit analysis.

### Comparative evaluation methods

This is a combination of different methods that compare the performance with that of the other co-workers. The usual techniques used may be ranking and paired comparison.

**Ranking:** The superior ranks his subordinate based on merit, from best to worst. However, how best and why best are not elaborated in this method. It is easy to administer and explain.

**Paired comparison:** In this method, each employee is rated with another employee in the form of pairs.

## Future-oriented Methods

### Management by objectives

This means that the performance is rated against the achievement of objectives stated by the management. This process includes:

- establishing goals and desired outcomes for each subordinate.
- setting performance standards.

- comparison of actual goals with the goals attained by the employee.
- establishing new goals and new strategies for goals not achieved in the previous year.

**Advantage:** It is more useful for managerial positions.

**Disadvantages:** Not applicable to all jobs; it may result in setting short-term goals rather than important long-term goals etc.

## Psychological appraisals

These appraisals are directed more to assessing employees' potential for future performance rather than the past one. It is done in the form of in-depth interviews, psychological tests, discussion with supervisors and review of other evaluations.

**Advantages:** It is more focused on employees' emotional, intellectual, motivational and other personal characteristics that affect his performance.

**Disadvantages:** This approach is slow and costly, and may be useful for bright young members who may have considerable potential. However, the quality of these appraisals largely depends on the skills of the psychologists, who perform the evaluation.

## Assessment centres

This technique was developed in the US and the UK in 1940s. An assessment centre is a central location where managers may come together to participate in job-related exercises evaluated by trained observers. It is more focused on observation of behaviours across a series of carefully selected exercises or work samples. Those being assessed are requested to participate in the in-basket exercises, work groups, computer simulations, role-playing and other similar activities, which require the same attributes for successful performance in actual job situations. The characteristics assessed may include assertiveness, persuasive ability, communication skills, planning and organisational skills, self-confidence, resistance to stress, energy level, decision making, sensitivity to feelings, administrative ability, creativity and mental alertness etc.

**Advantages:** Well-conducted assessment centres can achieve better forecasts of future performance and progress than other methods of appraisals. Reliability, content validity and predictive ability are said to be high in assessment centres. Tests ensure that the wrong people are not hired or promoted. This method clearly defines the criteria for selection and promotion.

**Disadvantages:** The organisation will have to bear the cost of employees' travelling and lodging, and psychologists. Besides, ratings may be strongly influenced by assessee's interpersonal skills. Solid performers may feel suffocated in simulated situations, while those who are not selected for these exercises may also get affected.

### The 360-degree feedback

This is a systematic collection of performance data of an individual group, derived from a number of stakeholders including immediate supervisors, team members, customers, peers and self. In fact anyone who has useful information on how an employee does a job may be one of the appraisers.

**Advantages:** This technique is highly useful in terms of getting a broader perspective, greater self-development and multi-source feedback. The 360-degree appraisal is useful for measuring interpersonal skills, customer satisfaction and team-building skills.

**Disadvantages:** Receiving feedback from multiple sources can be intimidating and threatening. Multiple raters may be less adept at providing balanced and objective feedback.

# 6

# Training For
# Appraisal

Training and development tools ensure that managers conduct performance appraisals effectively. This involves designing the process, training employees on how to use the tools, training managers on how to provide feedback and setting performance goals while adhering to legal guidelines. Comprehensive performance appraisal training and development enables organisations to validate that their employees have the right skills and knowledge to complete the tasks assigned to them and produce quality products and services. This is a process of quality assurance.

Training and development activities designed to support an effective performance appraisal process involve establishing an ongoing communication process between employees and managers. Learning how to define job responsibilities, competencies and performance measures ensures that the performance appraisal process works to improve employee achievement.

An effective performance appraisal process aids management in decision-making processes associated with promotion, discipline and salary administration. Dealing with performance problems promptly, avoids long-term issues including legal liabilities. Designing a customised performance appraisal programme and training the staff is important. Improved employee performance reduces mistakes, increases productivity and motivates all personnel to achieve strategic goals.

## TRAINING

### Types Of Training

Workshops and short sessions typically provide enough time to convey the key concepts about performance appraisal processes. Distance-learning alternatives allow employees located at different facilities to participate in the same session. Events can be recorded and archived for future access. In this way, all employees receive the same consistent message.

### Topics For Training

Performance appraisal training and development sessions for managers typically cover: what to say when conducting a performance review. Through role-play exercises, managers learn to clearly convey any goals that need adjustment to changing strategic objectives. Managers learn to reinforce the need for improving skills to enable high performance. They also learn to encourage and reward employees' strengths.

### Expert Insight

Performance appraisal training should ensure that employees are encouraged to take on more complex roles.

Gaps in training should lead to development or procurement of those courses that develop the required skills. Employees should be given definitive recommendations on how performance can be improved, such as starting or stopping certain behaviours. Creating a positive relationship with employees regarding performance improvement builds trust and enables growth and development, which benefits the company as a whole.

Training will empower one to:

- understand the benefits of performance management as a crucial management vehicle for achieving organisational goals.
- have a basic understanding of performance management including related tools and techniques.
- know how to develop/formulate goals, objectives, KPIs, competencies and performance standards.
- be able to utilise these generic performance interviewing skills.
  - Effective listening (including body language and tone of voice)
  - Giving constructive feedback (praise and constructive criticism)
  - Facilitating through questions
  - Responding with empathy
  - Handling difficult appraisees
- conduct an effective performance appraisal that would include:
  - planning and preparing for the appraisal.

- conducting the appraisal (facilitating agreement on actual performance and ratings for each performance measure).
- identifying environmental barriers that affect performance.
- identifying appraisee's training and development needs and completing a POP.
- following up.

## PERFORMANCE APPRAISAL BY LINE MANAGER

### Benefits To The Organisation

- Facilitates the achievement of organisational goals and strategies
- Contributes to improved staff morale
- Facilitates continuous performance improvement, organisation's development and culture change
- Assists in establishing a performance culture of quality, efficiency and achievement
- Provides a formal means of discussing competency gaps and how to address them, leading to a more competent workforce
- Helps build a climate of openness and trust
- Adds to a participative work culture
- Forms part of the legal process in addressing persistent poor performance
- Provides the basis for fair remuneration based on actual performance, so employees can see and experience a

clear link between their performance and the financial rewards they receive

## Benefits To Employees

- An opportunity to get formal feedback from line managers on their performance, so that they can learn what they do well and what needs to be improved.

- Ensures clarity regarding work expectations and standards, reducing anxiety/stress and conflict with line managers

- An opportunity to discuss their job competencies or lack thereof, leading to targeted training and development; thus helping them to realise their full potential

- Provides a forum to share new ideas and to air views

**Note:** Training in 'effectively conducting performance appraisals/reviews' will reduce line manager's reluctance and fear to do these with their direct reports. If done well, stress and conflict during the appraisal are greatly reduced.

# 7

# Dos And Don'ts

Performance review systems are sometimes designed and conducted in a way that they actually do more harm than good.

## TEN COMMON MISTAKES AND SOLUTIONS

**Mistake:** Performance review is a one-way top-down process in which the boss alone is the judge and jury of employees' behaviour and achievements on the job.

**Solution:** Make it a two-way process at the very least.

**Mistake:** Review process serves as a coaching tool for employee development as well as a compensation tool to decide salary increases.

**Solution:** Performance reviews should be done for either development or for compensation—not both.

**Mistake:** The person doing the appraisal has little or no day-to-day contact with the employee whose performance is being judged.

**Solution:** The person having review conversations with an employee should be the supervisor or manager who has the most contact with that employee and is in the best position to accurately assess his/her performance.

**Mistake:** Employees receive little or no advance notice of their 'reckoning day'.

**Solution:** Performance discussions ideally should be conducted on a regular basis, on a schedule well known and well publicised to everyone in the organisation.

**Mistake:** Managers are vague in their feedback to employees, or they assign arbitrary numerical 'grades' with little or no substantiation.

**Solution:** Performance feedback needs to be well documented in order to be effective; documentation should be done of both good and not-so-good results.

**Mistake:** The review process tries to evaluate traits, rather than behaviours and results.

**Solution:** Instead of traits, keep your evaluation focused on two things: behaviours and results.

**Mistake:** The appraisal is a once-a-year event that everyone tries to get through as quickly as they can, because it's painful for bosses and employees alike.

**Solution:** The primary goal in evaluating performance is to improve it. Therefore, you want to design a meaningful system of coaching conversations that people welcome, find useful, and deem valuable. Employees need regular feedback.

**Mistake:** There is no investigation of the causes that affect employees' performance.

**Solution:** People don't perform poorly for no reason. There are always causes—identify them.

**Mistake:** There is no follow-up action plan put in place at the end of the performance appraisal.

**Solution:** The final thing to discuss in a performance review conversation is 'What next?' Discuss what steps the employee needs to take to make sure that areas for improvement actually improve.

**Mistake:** Any attempt at pay-for-performance is ineffective because the difference in pay for a top performer and a mediocre performer is so small as to be meaningless.

**Solution:** If you can't come up with real money for real pay-for-performance, don't do it at all. It's better to give everyone the same percentage increase.

# 8

# Managing Appraisals

### Clarity Of Objectives

Ensure that you and your team members are clear about your individual roles and objectives. This will give the team a better context and perspective. This will also give you a foundation for setting goals.

### Keep At It

Schedule your appraisals once every six months to be sure that your team members are all pulling in the same direction, with monthly or bi-monthly reviews in between. This will help you avoid turn-turtle surprises.

**Remember:** Don't wait for an appraisal to tackle poor performance.

### Listen

Say less; listen more. Give the appraisee an opportunity to talk. They should be speaking more than you.

## Simple Rapport Techniques

Simple rapport techniques will help; so be positive and encourage the appraisee to speak. The meeting should be held where there are little or no interruptions and distractions. Switch off your phone. Don't check your emails. Follow a simple rule: smile and make eye contact.

## Smart: Targets, KPIs And Objectives

Make the targets, KPIs and objectives SMART: Specific, Measurable, Achievable, Realistic and Timely. Augur a well-defined company vision that is known and understood by all personnel; use the appraisal to reinforce these values. Working as a group, towards a common goal, is a powerful motivator!

## Limit The Appraisal To Three/Four Key Things

Keep it simple. Limit it to a few factors; avoid long lists of points.

## Be Objective

Reflect on the performance of each team member as objectively as possible.

## Requests For A Pay Rise, Training Or Promotion

Avoid pressure. Probe for reasons and examples to support the request and take the information away for consideration.

## Turn Negatives Into Positives

If you need to be critical or discuss poor performance, be clear and constructive. Make your point and support it with examples. Turn the negative points into positive with a planned framework for improved performance and assure the individual that this is something you can work through together.

**Appraisal Notes**

Write them quickly while everything is fresh in your mind. Ensure that all points are agreed by both parties and ideally signed by all involved. Appraisal notes should be kept confidential.

**The Bottom Line:** At the end of the discussion, recapitulate the salient points so there is no room for misinterpretation.

# 9

# Pitfalls In Appraisals

### Expectations Galore

Appraisals often try to accomplish too many things. Managers are expected to justify merit increases, give feedback, document performance problems and provide career counselling. If money is part of the discussion, one objective undermines the other.

### Bureaucratic Attitude And Constraints Of Time

Depending on the method used, some performance appraisals are complex, involve bureaucratic forms and take too much of managers' time.

### Timing

Many companies conduct reviews based on the employees' date of employment anniversary or on a pre-selected date that matches an administrative time-line. While such timing may make sense on one level, consider this: would it make sense to evaluate Father Christmas in June or a cricket player on his birthday?

## Could Be Demoralising At Times

Few of us enjoy hearing about our shortcomings and few managers enjoy discussing them. When you consider that 80 per cent of employees believe they're in the top quarter of all workers, it's easy to see why a once- or twice-a-year evaluation is believed to be demoralising.

## Legal Considerations

Companies document performance feedback. Most employers know that should they face a wrongful termination suit, the employee's attorney would immediately seek a record of performance appraisals. Employers who are prudent about the law will document performance problems.

## A Model

The management must decide precisely what it wants to achieve with performance appraisals. It should design a practical system that meets those goals, keeping in mind the precious commodities of time and money.

An effective system involves many factors, but these two are among the most important.

### *Frequency of appraisals*

It is expected that workers be project driven and result oriented. For this, feedback is essential. Feedback delayed for up to a year is useless for an employee and can be disastrous for a company. In the fast-paced business world, the best managers spend, on an average, about one hour per person per quarter discussing performance. In between conversational meetings devoted to feedback, managers can build helpful interactions through routine meetings and can deliver feedback through voicemail, email or short notes. Regularity of feedback eases the anxiety inherent in being at firing line on an under-performing employee during an annual review.

### Raising and feedback levels

Again, performance appraisals that attempt to accomplish everything in one meeting are bound to disappoint. A discussion of money nearly always overshadows everything else covered in the meeting. Employees hear only 'how much' and cannot focus on their performance. Companies, with frequent feedback and performance planning sessions, allot separate times each year to discuss further feedback.

## TYPES OF APPRAISAL

Performance appraisal deals with how organisations evaluate and measure employees' achievements and behaviours. It is an employee's review by his manager where his work performance is evaluated and strengths and weaknesses are identified so that the employee knows his improvement areas. Performance appraisal is the right time to set new goals and objectives for employees. It allows the management to categorise employees into performers and non-performers. This is primarily done to estimate employees' worth.

There are variations of performance appraisal systems.

## Behavioural Checklist

Behavioural checklist has a list of criterion that an employee should work on, in order to be a diligent worker. The behaviours differ according to the type of job assessed. This method is considered favourable as the evaluation is done on the basis of individual employee performance without comparisons.

## 360-Degree Appraisal

A 360-degree appraisal involves feedback of the manager, supervisor, team members and any direct reports. In this method of appraisal, the employee's complete profile has to be compiled and assessed. In addition to evaluating the employee's work performance and technical skill set, an appraiser collects an in-depth feedback of the employee.

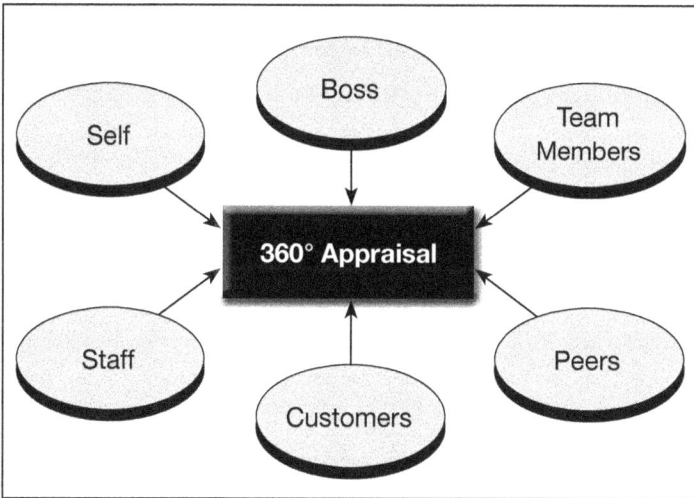

**Management By Objective**

In this method of performance appraisal, the manager and the employee agree upon specific and attainable goals with a set deadline. With this method, the appraiser can define success and failure easily.

**Insight Appraisals**

This appraisal method evaluates employees' intellect, emotional stability, analytical skills and other psychological traits. This method makes it easy for the manager to place employees in appropriate teams.

# 10

# Performance Appraisal

## PERFORMANCE APPRAISAL

A performance appraisal (PA), also known as a performance review, performance evaluation (career) development discussion or an employee appraisal, is a method by which the job performance of an employee is documented and evaluated. Performance appraisals are part of career development and consist of regular reviews of employee performance within organisations.

A performance appraisal is a systematic and periodic process that assesses an individual's performance and productivity in relation to certain pre-established criteria and organisational objectives.

## COLLECTING PERFORMANCE APPRAISAL DATA

There are three main methods to collect PA data.

- Objective production
- Personnel
- Judgemental evaluation

Judgmental evaluations are most commonly used with a large variety of evaluation methods.

**Time frame:** It could be every six months, every quarter, weekly or bi-weekly. The interview could aim at:

- providing feedback to employees.
- counselling and developing employees.
- conveying and discussing compensation and job status.
- taking disciplinary decisions.

PA is often included in performance management systems. PA helps the subordinate to answer two key questions.

- What are your expectations of me?
- How am I going to meet your expectations?

How performance is managed in an organisation determines to a large extent the success or failure of the organisation. Therefore, improving PA should be among the highest priorities of contemporary organisations.

Applications of PA:

- Compensation
- Performance improvement
- Promotions
- Termination
- Test validation

## Benefits Of Performance Appraisal

- There are a number of potential benefits of performance appraisals. It often leads to positive implications for organisations. PAs can benefit an organisation's effectiveness. It is an effective way of giving workers feedback about their job performance. This can lead to individual workers becoming more productive.

- Feedback and management–employee communication can serve as a guide in job performance. Such communication in organisations is a means to motivate the worker. It removes perceptions of uncertainty.

- It can make the employees develop trust. PAs have the ability to encourage trust within the organisation.

- It is a tool to align individual worker's goals and performance with organisational goals. PAs provide and encourage discussion through collaboration of these individual and organisational goals; they become 'partners in progress.'

- This helps determine training needs. In fact this leads to post-appraisal opportunities for training and development in problem areas.

**Drawbacks Of Performance Appraisal**

PA may result in legal issues if not executed appropriately. Determining the relationship between individual job performance and organisational performance can be a Herculean task. It can also be detrimental to the organisation if the appraisals are not used appropriately. It can be detrimental to quality improvement. Subjective evaluations are not an issue. They are often based on a manager's or supervisor's perceptions of an employee's performance and employees are evaluated subjectively rather than objectively.

Sometimes reviews may be influenced by many non-performance factors, such as:

- employee 'likeability',
- personal prejudices,
- ease of management, and
- previous mistakes or successes.

Negative perceptions can be distressing. They can cause tension between supervisors and subordinates. If the person being appraised does not trust the employer/appraiser or believes that he will benefit from the process, it may become a veritable Pandora's box exercise.

Reviews should instead be based on data-supported measurable behaviours and results that are within the performer's control. PA should provide accurate and relevant ratings of an employee's performance as compared to pre-established criteria/goals. Inflated ratings are a common malady. Goals may at times be overly challenging or over-emphasised to the extent of affecting quality.

## IMPROVING PERFORMANCE APPRAISAL

### Training

Creating an awareness and acceptance in the people conducting appraisals that within a group of workers they will find wide differences in skills and abilities.

### Providing Feedback To Raters

Trained raters provide managers, who evaluate their subordinates, with feedback, including information on ratings from other managers.

## Subordinate Participation

Allowing employee participation in the evaluation process will end discrepancies between self-ratings and supervisor ratings. This will increase job satisfaction and motivation.

## STAKEHOLDERS

## Managers

Managers with inadequate or poorly designed appraisal programmes may be sceptical about their usefulness.

- Some managers may not like to play the role of a judge and be responsible for the future of their subordinates.
- They may be uncomfortable about providing negative feedback to employees.
- This tendency can lead them to inflate their assessment of workers' job performance, giving higher ratings than deserved.

## Peers

Peer ranking requires each group member to rank all fellow members from 'best' to 'worst' on one or more dimensions of performance.

**Self-assessment:** Individuals assess and evaluate their own behaviour and job performance.

**Peer assessment:** Members of a group evaluate and appraise the performance of their fellow group members.

**360-degree feedback:** A 360-degree feedback involves multiple evaluations of an employee's performance, which often includes assessment from superior(s), peers and self.

## PERFORMANCE APPRAISAL INTERVIEWS

Performance appraisal interview is the final step of the appraisal process. The interview is held between the subordinate and supervisor. The interview is of great significance to an organisation's PA system. The superior and subordinate participate in the interview discussion and establish goals together.

These three factors consistently contribute to effective PA interviews.

- Supervisor's knowledge of the subordinate's job and performance in it
- Supervisor's support of the subordinate
- Welcoming of the subordinate's participation

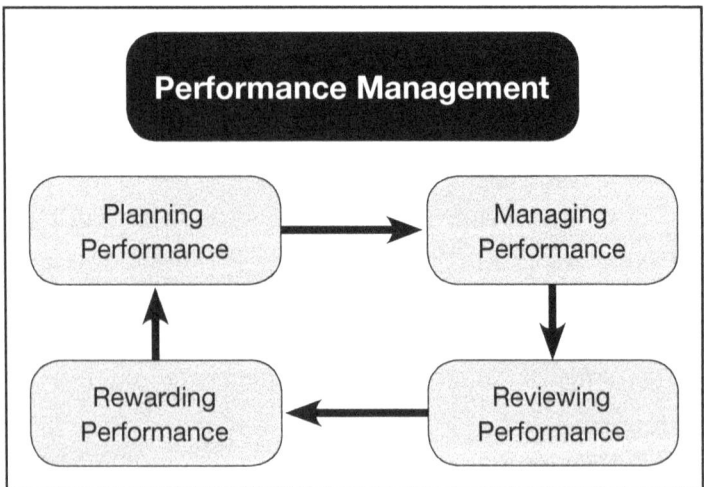

# 11

# Tips For An Effective Performance Review

Performance reviews should be: positive, valuable assessments that lead to maximising staff performance, and able to help employees achieve their professional goals and the organisation's objectives.

## Performance Review Guide -
*Tips to write, prepare and ask*

**Tip 1**

Don't just rely on your memory when writing employee reviews. Do document employee performance before writing employee reviews; maintain a log for each employee. Performance logs don't need to be complicated or sophisticated. They can simply be paper files in a folder or computer files.

**Tip 2**

Conduct a positive, valuable employee performance evaluation. Don't make the process tense or uncomfortable. Begin by discussing any problems you've observed with the employee's performance. Address each problem individually and don't bring up a new problem until you've thoroughly discussed the current one. Use this framework to discuss each problem.

- Describe the performance problem

- Reinforce performance standards

- Develop a plan for improvement

- Offer your help

- Alternate negative and positive comments

- Emphasise on potential

## Tip 3

Turn a negative into a positive: During performance reviews, use clear, non-judgemental language that focuses on results and behaviour.

## Tip 4

Measure an employee's 'intangible' traits.

- Match traits to the job
- Match traits to behaviour

You can't help being subjective when evaluating intangible factors. But you can avoid bias by focusing on concrete instances in which the employee displayed positive or negative behaviour regarding a particular trait.

## Tip 5

Avoid phrases in the employee performance evaluation that can sabotage job-review meetings. Don't unintentionally communicate the wrong message or come across as too negative or personal. This may hurt the employee's morale, weaken productivity or lead the organisation into a discrimination lawsuit.

### Tip 6

Help employees reach their peak performance. Expect high performance and you won't be disappointed. Expect so-so performance and that's what you'll get. Involve them in setting goals. Then negotiate your expectations, but keep the goals realistic. Avoid micromanaging.

### Tip 7

Job reviews shouldn't be paper-moving programmes that return zero value.

### Tip 8

While writing employee reviews, steer clear of these errors.

- Evaluating attitude, not performance. Never use the word 'attitude' when writing employee reviews.

- Evaluating inflation. Supervisors too often rate mediocre employees as competent; competent employees as above average; and above-average employees as superior. Beware!

### Tip 9

Incorporate self-review (by employee) and reinvent the employee performance evaluation system.

TIME FOR REVIEW

**Tip 10**

Simplify. Write the employee review.

## PERFECT ASSERTIVENESS

Assertiveness is important in all forms of communication. It is a way of relating to others that respects both your own and other people's needs, wants and rights. Aggressiveness provokes counter-aggression, assertiveness doesn't. *Perfect Assertiveness* spells out:

- Assertiveness training
- Responses: Passive, aggressive and assertive
- Effective communication
- Assertiveness skills
- Benefits of being assertive

*Perfect Assertiveness* helps you understand assertiveness as a life skill.

## PERFECT COMMUNICATION

Communication is the process of sharing information, knowledge or meaning. What matters most is the 'response-ability'; response is more important than the message. Listeners must not just hear; they must listen. *Perfect Communication* deals with:

- Speaking skills
- Writing skills
- Listening skills

*Perfect Communication* is much more than just this.

## PERFECT CV

A curriculum vitae (CV) or résumé presents a record of your qualities, skills and experience to an employer, so that your suitability for a particular job can be assessed. In Latin, 'curriculum vitae' means 'the way your life has run' and 'résumé' is the French word for 'summary'. *Perfect CV* deals with:

- Making a CV special
- Writing a CV with lack of experience
- Tailoring a CV
- Digital CVs
- Online CVs

*Perfect CV* helps you to compile your CV and suggests ways to improve it.


## PERFECT LEADER

If you want to inspire, motivate and engage, and move people into action, leadership is the ability you require. Leaders set direction and develop the skill to guide people to the right destination. *Perfect Leader* spells out:

- Leadership styles
- Initiatives that are needed
- Proactive tools
- The importance of perseverance
- Methods to step out of the comfort zone

*Perfect Leader* helps you to inspire the vision of the future as a leader. It equips you to make strategic decisions, shape conflict and find your competitive edge.

# PERFECT MEETING

Meetings help one to build rapport. They are a forum for inter-learning and understanding; a platform to share information. *Perfect Meeting* is about the basic skills of management. It deals with:

- Effective meetings
- Conference meetings
- Stand-up meetings
- One-on-one meetings
- Tasks and skills of the chairperson

*Perfect Meeting* helps you generate cooperation and commitment to attain higher levels of performance.

# PERFECT NEGOTIATION

In order to settle differences, one needs to master the skill of negotiation. Without this skill, conflicts and disagreements will arise. *Perfect Negotiation* deals with the process of negotiation and its different stages.

- Preparation
- Discussion
- Goals
- Win-win outcome
- Agreement

*Perfect Negotiation* helps you master the different types of negotiation formats, styles, and preparing strategies for negotiation.